LIFE 101:
21 PRACTICAL PERSONAL GROWTH PRINCIPLES FOR THE 21ST CENTURY

ASHLEY ANNE CONNOLLY, M.ED., LPC

BALBOA.
PRESS
A DIVISION OF HAY HOUSE

Balboa Press books may be ordered through booksellers or by contacting:

Balboa Press
A Division of Hay House
1663 Liberty Drive
Bloomington, IN 47403
www.balboapress.com
1 (877) 407-4847

Because of the dynamic nature of the Internet, any web addresses or links contained in this book may have changed since publication and may no longer be valid. The views expressed in this work are solely those of the author and do not necessarily reflect the views of the publisher, and the publisher hereby disclaims any responsibility for them.

The author of this book does not dispense medical advice or prescribe the use of any technique as a form of treatment for physical, emotional, or medical problems without the advice of a physician, either directly or indirectly. The intent of the author is only to offer information of a general nature to help you in your quest for emotional and spiritual well-being. In the event you use any of the information in this book for yourself, which is your constitutional right, the author and the publisher assume no responsibility for your actions.

Any people depicted in stock imagery provided by Thinkstock are models, and such images are being used for illustrative purposes only. Certain stock imagery © Thinkstock.

Print information available on the last page.

ISBN: 978-1-5043-4486-9 (sc)
ISBN: 978-1-5043-4488-3 (hc)
ISBN: 978-1-5043-4487-6 (e)

Library of Congress Control Number: 2015957569

Balboa Press rev. date: 12/14/2015

To Mike...who lives these principles.

INTRODUCTION

Congratulations! Because you are reading these words you are about to embark on a journey of discovering useful principles for optimal well-being. **Life 101** is a simple, concise, practical and effective tool for people who want to learn basic personal growth principles in a hands-on and straight-forward format. This succinct manuscript is designed for the Millennial age; where we are accustomed to getting information quickly, efficiently and in a practical manner, i.e. Twitter, Facebook, Instagram.

I majored in psychology in college hoping to learn basic, useful principles about how to live a happy and purposeful life, but instead found heavy philosophy and often useless theories mostly written by long-dead men. Psychology has a long tradition of focusing on pathology rather than wellness. While the emerging field of Positive Psychology is changing that dynamic, there nevertheless remains undue focus on pathological behavior and less emphasis on techniques for a normal individual to find strategies to live their best life. **Life 101** focuses on maximizing your potential and optimizing your wellness.

And why am I the person to write this book? Just ask my husband. Our bookshelves are chock-full of every sort of self-help, personal growth, and spiritual growth book you can imagine. I am in long-term recovery, a self-help devotee, a long-term student of A Course in Miracles, Science of Mind, Self -Realization Fellowship and other religious and spiritual traditions, and have attended countless self-help step meetings. I have graduate and undergraduate degrees in psychology and advanced training in transpersonal psychology. In addition, I am a licensed psychotherapist with a private practice and extensive experience working in a variety of capacities in the mental health field.

Life 101 is designed to be read as a simple manual for how to live the best life that you are capable of living. What I have come to find is that the content of the many different source materials I have consulted in my unconscious attempt at becoming a self-help guru ultimately contain very similar messages. Emotional wellness does not have to be complicated! There are very simple and effective methods to live in a state of well-being. I won't try to pretend that anything I am writing is an original thought, as these basic ideas have been expounded and expanded upon by numerous luminaries over the years. But the voice is mine and the straightforward interpretation of lofty principles and ideals is my attempt to make personal growth and self-improvement possible for anyone and everyone, simply and effectively.

Open your mind. Take a deep breath. And get ready to begin the journey of becoming a conscious creator of your life. Thank you. Namaste.

In love and light,
Ashley Connolly, M.Ed., LPC – September 2015

Principle 1

Thoughts Are Everything!

"Folks are usually about as happy as they make their minds to be."
-Abraham Lincoln

From New Age books, academic psychology journals, to Western and Eastern spiritual traditions; the message is the same – **pay attention to your thoughts, and then choose good ones**. The basic premise behind nearly all effective 'self-help', spiritual or psychological programs is the very basic idea that 1) our thoughts create our emotions, 2) that very often these (negative) thoughts are not true, so 3) to change the way we feel we need to change our thoughts.

The key is to examine our thoughts and to become conscious and aware of their content. Is your inner dialog kind? Do you speak to yourself in a loving manner? Honestly look at whether the ticker tape in your mind is a ticker tape of love or one of fear. Your self-talk ultimately determines your self-worth. Tell yourself you are beautiful, funny, joyful, happy, abundant, loving, good, worthy, satisfied – even if at the time you don't necessarily believe it. Change the inner dialog.

If you feel that your thoughts are not necessarily representative of self-love, complete this simple exercise. Choose three or four sentences from the list below (or write your own) and commit to memory. Any time you notice negative thoughts, stop and repeat your personal mantra out-loud or internally, even if at the time you don't believe it.

> *I am lovable.*
> *I am beautiful.*
> *All is well in my world.*
> *Life is good.*
> *I am joy.*
> *Joy overflows in my life.*
> *I love life.*
> *I love me.*
> *I am happy.*
> *I love everyone and everyone loves me.*
> *I am love.*
> *Love is everywhere.*

My personal mantra is "All is well. I am blessed. Life is good. Thank you God."

Positive thinking and reducing negative thoughts should not be construed to mean that you will never experience negative emotions. Sadness, grief and anger will still be experienced in small appropriate doses. The key is to make sure your thoughts are not distorted, and that what you are feeling is an appropriate response to a given situation. For example, 'I am feeling sad because my dog died.' is an appropriate response to loss. Telling yourself; 'I am the worst dog owner and I will never ever find a dog like Scruffy again and I will never ever feel better again because he is gone' is an example of an unhealthy thought process.

Your thoughts not only influence how you feel about yourself, but they also may have a very real impact on the outcomes that manifest in your life. Research is beginning to demonstrate that our thoughts may actually have creative powers. Whether or not if you think about your dream house, dream job, or dream man long-enough and with enough conviction, you will manifest it; is, in my opinion, beside the point. As far as I'm concerned, creating positive outcomes with our minds is simply a better way to spend an afternoon than worrying about outcomes. And it leads to optimal mental health! Creating specific outcomes may just be an added bonus. Worry is simply using your imagination to begin to create things you don't want.

Spend some time each day in your creative corner. Decide what you want, visualize it and start creating a whole fantasy world around this idea. Use the down times in your day: lines, traffic jams, computer starting up, teeth brushing, or showering to enter your own personal creative corner.

Thoughts are things. Choose yours wisely.

Principle 2

Do Esteemable Things

"The world won't care about your self-esteem. The world will expect you to accomplish something before you feel good about yourself." - Bill Gates

To get self-esteem, do 'esteemable' things. I should actually just end the chapter after that three word sentence; as that sentence really encompasses the very simple and effective means of increasing your self-esteem. It is a common, albeit, trite saying floating around self-help groups, that "To get self-esteem, do 'esteemable' things."

What does that mean? Basically it means acting with integrity and living your life so that your actions are aligned with your values. It means doing the right thing instead of the thing that feels good. It means helping others. It means taking time out of your day to reflect. It means conducting yourself in such a manner that your God would be proud of you. It means living your life in such a way that you wouldn't be afraid if the town gossip had access to your daily affairs.

A recipe for low self-esteem is to continue to do things that make you feel guilt and shame. Low self-esteem is a result of conducting yourself in a manner that you know, at a deep level, is not morally, ethically, spiritually or emotionally sound. It is awfully convenient and tempting to blame our low self-esteem on other people. Your parents were mean to you, nobody gave you unconditional love, your spouse yells at you, your boss berates you, you were teased in kindergarten; the list could go on and on.

And yes, there is some validity that we are programmed consciously and unconsciously with the messages we received at an early age and that we continue to hear. Don't give your power to others. You no longer have the luxury of blaming your problems and your low self-esteem on other people. You are in charge of your thoughts now.

The solution remains the same – start doing esteemable things. Be a good person. Give to others. If you remain in a relationship that reinforces your negative self-worth, you have the luxury and freedom of terminating the relationship. As they say in a co-dependent self-help program, "If you want to stop being treated like a doormat, get off the floor."

Get off the floor, let go of blame, and take responsibility for the content of your thoughts about yourself. The best way to feel good about yourself is to do things that make you proud of you. Often times people mistake trying to increase their self-esteem by doing things that feel good. For instance, having four glasses of wine, engaging in an illicit love affair, buying an expensive car, watching a mindless TV program, eating a bag of chips; these activities may feel good at the time but ultimately will not enhance your self-esteem. Conversely, running a marathon, helping a stranger fix a flat tire, sitting with a dying friend, donating money to a great cause, or volunteering for a non-profit, might not necessarily feel good in the moment, but will ultimately enhance your self-esteem.

This principle for living, doing what is good and not just what feels good, is a cornerstone for a happy life.

PRINCIPLE 3

People Are Difficult

"Be kind. For everyone you meet is fighting a hard battle." – Plato

Let go of expectations of others. Accept the fact that most people in this world, including ourselves; are emotionally fragile and very often wrong. We are all wounded in some way, shape or form. The problem lies in the fact that most of us expect other people to behave as psychologically mature, astute, reasonable and loving beings. Unfortunately, that is usually not the case. People are doing the best they can with the often limited emotional skills they possess.

Expectations are premeditated resentments. Expecting certain things from people ultimately leads to disillusionment and dissatisfaction. I don't recommend adopting an utterly pessimistic attitude about humankind, but a empathic and realistic assessments of others allows for fewer disappointments. Allow yourself to be pleasantly surprised by the graciousness of someone's behavior, instead of constantly let down.

In terms of other people's behaviors; as they say in co-dependent groups; you didn't cause it, you can't control it and you can't cure it. **Detach with love.** Allow others to make their own lives. **Live and let live.** Give your loved one the opportunity to grow from their mistakes. Enabling unhealthy behavior keeps them from ultimately experiencing the lesson they need so they don't have to repeat the pattern in an unhealthy way.

For the truly toxic relationships in your life, it is important to do some housecleaning. Those individuals who have continually shown you their brokenness and none of their graciousness - it is time to release those relationships with love. You need to value yourself enough to stop accepting unacceptable behavior. You teach people how to treat you. Sometimes the lesson for them is that people will no longer tolerate their unhealthy behavior. As Maya Angelou and Oprah preach, "When someone shows you who they are, believe them the first time."

Accept that other people may very often be wrong, but know that the ONLY thing you can do about it is to look at your part and clean up your side of the street. Twelve step programs encourage members to focus on "their part" of any given resentment. Where were you selfish, dishonest, self-seeking, unkind, or unloving? What would you do differently if you had to do it again? Do you owe an amends? How can you make things right in the relationship?

If you decide you want to mend a relationship and have accepted your part in the conflict, despite the fact that you have been wronged, these five sentences work wonders in healing.

> *I am sorry.*
> *I was wrong.*
> *Please forgive me.*
> *What can I do to make it up to you?*
> *I love you.*

Do not allow the opinion of an emotionally unstable person influence your self-worth. If a psychotic and delusional mental patient told you that you had were purple and that you were a covert alien spy, you would not let that assessment bring you down. Similarly, you should not allow the judgment of an equally mentally handicapped person impact your self-worth. As Don Miguel Ruiz states as one of his agreements in his classic book *The Four Agreements,* "Don't take things personally." The majority of what other people think of you has very little to do with you and everything to do with them.

Finally, I would like to provide you with an easy strategy to employ when in the presence of a difficult, demeaning and unkind person. Visualize a white light surrounding them and repeat internally over and over, "*May you be filled with loving kindness. May you know peace. May you be filled with loving-kindness. May you know love.*" It may not make them more peaceful, but it certainly will bring more peace into your own heart. But I believe (and have seen it work many times) that on some level they will feel the energy behind your intention and their attitude toward you will soften. I have been astounded to literally see energy shift in someone's demeanor when I mentally employ this tactic, shifting from distrustful to trusting, fearful to open, angry to conciliatory.

We are all beautiful and broken. Accept the brokenness. But know you don't have to live in it. Embrace the beauty.

PRINCIPLE 4

Act As If

"You can't think your way into right action,
but you can act your way into right thinking." – Bill Wilson

There is a saying in the 12 step and psychotherapy worlds known simply as 'Act as if.' 'Act as if' you didn't feel depressed, anxious, guilty, tired, angry, or any of the myriad negative emotions we can become attached to. Act as if you were happy, content, peaceful, satisfied, loved, serene and joyful. Sounds simple? It is.

The premise behind this notion is to lead with our actions, not our feelings. So you wake up feeling down and just want to stay in bed? Instead of following your feelings which tell you to pull the covers over your head, lead with your actions. Allow your feet to guide you into a better feeling mood. Get up, dress in a way that makes you feel good, get outside, take a walk, exercise, visit a friend. In short, do anything but what your sad and anxious feelings are telling you to do. We are not at mercy to our feelings.

Sometimes you really have to do some creative work to put this principle into action. Pretend you are in a movie and that you are cast as the lead; a person with a shiny, optimistic and sunny disposition. You can even give this alter-ego a name. Play with the idea. Get creative. You are allowed to be anything you want to be in this life. Why not choose to be a hero or a shero?

There is a secondary notion similar to 'acting as if' known as *contrary action*. The principle behind this is to act in the opposite manner of how we are feeling or what we are telling ourselves we should do. A great Seinfeld episode details this notion hysterically with George deciding to act opposite of his natural instinct. This idea is only useful if your previous actions have been harmful to your well-being. So if you feel like drinking, smoking, over-indulging, yelling, isolating or staying in bed all day, determine to do the opposite.

While I am not minimizing the very real stressors people may have in their life by not allowing for indulgences in self-pity, this idea is simply one more tool to add to your self-help tool-box. (For those suffering from clinical depression or any other severe disorders, sometimes self-help is not enough and professional help or God-help is in order – more on that in later chapters.)

'Act as if' prescription = *Picture yourself as the happiest person in the world.* Then conduct your business of the day as if you were that person.

PRINCIPLE 5

Be Your Own Best Friend

"It's not your job to like me. It's mine." -Byron Katie

Be your own best friend, therapist, sister, brother, mentor, mother, spouse, father or God. Think of the people in your life who absolutely love you unconditionally (and please note that the above mentioned people may or may not be people that actually do love you unconditionally). Then think about what they would say about you in terms of your good qualities or what advice they might give you in any given situation.

Whenever you are in the midst of internal emotional abuse, stop and reflect upon what your loved one might have to say about your assessment of yourself. Would they say those cruel things about you that are running through your mind? Probably not.

We need to see us as *Unconditional Love* sees us. So the best eyes to view through are the eyes of those people who love us. If you have a relationship with a Higher Power or God, think about how your personal God views you. The Divine Mind or Unconditional Love is probably a lot more compassionate about your mistakes and your perceived physical, emotional and mental flaws then you are.

We can also use these relationships in our lives to have imaginary conversations with ourselves to solve any given problem, or if you can't actually solve the problem, then to change your negative self-talk about the situation. Learning to step outside your mind and to become a witness to your own life is one of the highest forms of psychological functioning.

Often, when a friend presents us with a problem, we are pretty clear of the solution, and if we have unconditional love towards this person, we also see how their negative self-talk is futile. For instance, imagine if your best friend, whom you love and support wholeheartedly, comes to you crying. She states that her boyfriend just hit her and locked her out of the house and is crying about how she is unworthy, unlovable, stupid and unattractive. It would be awfully easy to provide her with the verbal reassurances to counter-act the negative self-assessment.

The key is to be that kind to ourselves! Maybe the situation won't be quite as dramatic, but after a poor work evaluation and not getting a promotion you feel defeated, disappointed and worthless, try being your own advocate. Put yourselves literally in the mind-set of your favorite cheerleader and actually think about what they would say to you. Find a few phrases they might use and begin repeating them internally.

Our brains are designed to work, so unless you are an advanced yogi or Buddhist meditator, your mind is going to buzz. The mind abhors silence and a vacuum, so for most of us we need something to fill the void where our negative self-critical voice often speaks up. Filling your head with the kind and loving voices of the people who love you unconditionally will provide yet another tool to add to your self-help bag of tricks.

Principle 6

Denial Can Be Your Friend

"Denial is a useful defense mechanism
until it's not." – Rosalind Kaplan

Just because something bad happened to you, it does not mean that you automatically are going to be traumatized by the situation and are going to suffer years and years of misery. Denial is a defense mechanism that actually can serve a very healthy purpose. Defense mechanisms are useful for a time but get a bad rap because ultimately, for some people, severe psychological symptoms can come to the surface if left unresolved.

For example, someone who was verbally abused may wind up with extreme low self-esteem and clinical anxiety. This individual may in fact need to go back and really work through the past trauma and upset with a professional in order to release the pain from the past to ultimately achieve emotional stability. It isn't always the case, however, that one needs to rehash the past pain in order to heal.

In this day and age of self-help, armchair therapists and Google diagnoses; many people feel that just because they went through something upsetting that they are doomed to experience clinical symptoms. For instance, I have had several clients walk into my office with a self-diagnosis of Post-Traumatic Stress Disorder, (PTSD) because they experienced a recent trauma and PTSD is often reported in the media. More often than not, they are experiencing a natural reaction to trauma and not the clinical symptoms of a real diagnosis. What I help them work through is the fact that yes, they are experiencing some normal emotional pain from the trauma, but they don't actually meet the clinical criteria of a full-blown mental disorder. Similarly, I have known many a young women to diagnose themselves with an eating disorder, when what presents clinically is merely a quite typical women that worries a bit too much about her weight and what she puts into her body. Labels can disempower us and keep us in a state of victim-hood.

The truth is that for most of us we really do NOT have to process fully every bad thing that has ever happened to us! Our emotional system is actually very effective at helping us to cope with the trials of life. It is only when negative symptoms arise that we need to look at where we may have been hurt in the past and what we may need to heal and work through in therapy. As the old saying goes, "if it ain't broke, don't fix it."

There is a disturbing trend among young people in particular to identify with their diagnoses and victimhood. We have made tremendous positive strides in terms of de-stigmatizing mental illness, but I fear that we have gone too far in the other direction and many vulnerable souls have taken up their emotional wounds as their personal badges of honor.

Remember, denial can be your friend. If you don't have any symptoms, you can simply let the past trauma stay there. So when you hear people tell you things like, "It takes half as many years as you were with a person to get over the relationship before you can move on.", or "Grief lasts at least a year.", "You need to deal with your Daddy issues" or other such well-meaning advice, smile and nod and ask yourself if you really need to relive your pain, or if you want to take a step in the direction of a bright future instead.

If you do find you need to spend some time in your grief and sadness; that is ok. Just know you do not need to stay there and that it is not an automatic fact that you must feel sad for "x" amount of time or because you experienced "x", you will automatically feel "y". You have the freedom to choose your own emotions and to begin again at any moment. And if you find yourself worried because you feel like you 'should' be more upset than you are, stop and congratulate yourself and express gratitude for your healthy emotional compass system. Then you can simply move on towards the directions of your dreams in joy, peace, gratitude and love.

PRINCIPLE 7

Don't Take Life So Seriously

*"The human race has one really effective weapon
and that is laughter." – Mark Twain*

Self-help 12-step groups have something they refer to cryptically as "Rule #62". Upon examination, one discovers that Rule #62 is an arbitrary number, as there are no "rules" in 12 step programs and it simply means, "Don't Take Yourself So Seriously." I imagine the original idea behind the gag was that people would get all worked up emotionally worrying about what others referred to as the 62nd rule, obviously thinking there were 61 other rules they didn't know about. In reality, there are no rules and this playful rule was designed to remind us all to lighten up.

Have you ever been tremendously worried about something only to completely forget about it the next day, week, or month? Have you ever noticed how often the things you worry about never come to pass? Have you ever agonized over something only to realize upon later reflection how cosmically unimportant it was? Embrace the possibility that this world is really just one big cosmic playground. Imagine that your life and your choices are simply a part of the beautiful ebb and flow of the universe and matter not much more than how a child plays on the playground. Provided you act with integrity and do no harm, ultimately your life is simply one more drama on the cosmic stage.

Whenever you find yourself in an agitated emotional state, stop and ask yourself the following questions: *Will this issue matter at all in one years' time? Is this issue really important to my values? If this situation turns out in the worst case scenario, would I get through it?*

For example, imagine you are emotionally distraught because a respected professor criticized your work and gave you a terrible grade. Of course, the natural human instinct is to feel upset and to personalize. But put it to the long-term importance test and see how quickly and easily you can realize just how unimportant this situation is in the long-term.

Don't take life so seriously. Don't take yourself so seriously. Give everything the long-range check. Will it matter in a year? Usually not.

Principle 8

Find a Faith That Works For You

"Belief is a wise wager. Granted that faith cannot be proved, what harm will come to you if you gamble on its truth and it proves false? If you gain, you gain all; if you lose, you lose nothing. Wager, then, without hesitation, that He exists."
Blaise Pascal

Faith works. Research shows that people that have a faith in Something, most call it God, are healthier, happier and maintain better relationships. Faith is not religion. Faith is not dogma. Faith is not attendance at church or membership in any group. Faith is your own answer to the question: *Is there a Loving Power greater than me and is it acting in my life to assist me?* If you answer yes to that question, than consider yourself fortunate.

If you answered no or you are uncertain whether you believe there is a higher meaning in your life, consider the possibility of just choosing to believe just for the very sake of feeling better. My Grandmother used to say, "I wish I could believe in heaven just like all my friends, as it would be a nice comfort." What I have always thought is, 'why don't *you just choose to believe then?*' We choose other things in life – where we are going to live, our career, our life partner, our friends – why can't we simply choose to believe in a personal God and a spiritual world that works for us?

Consider the possibility that believing is as simple as making a decision to believe. If it makes us feel better to believe there is a Loving Presence helping out and watching over us and loving us unconditionally and that there is a loving, light, beautiful spirit world where we transition upon our death, why don't we just choose to believe, even if we don't know how or why It exists?

Self-help groups like AA encourage their members to choose their own conception of God. Sponsors will sometimes ask sponsees to write a "Want Ad' for the kind of Higher Power they would want working in their life. Then they tell the baffled newcomer, 'that's it – there's your Higher Power'. The fact of the matter is that NO ONE, not the most studied theologian, the most devout monk, revered minister, popular televangelist or devoted disciple really knows the answer to life's biggest questions and how and why God exists or doesn't exist. So choose your own faith that works for you. Make a decision to believe.

You don't have to understand how God works in your life in order to get benefit from It's results. Just as I really don't understand how the Internet works, how my car starts and how my television turns on when I push a button; I nevertheless believe that they will work as they have in the past and I rely on them to do the things I want them to do. So it is with your Higher Power.

Ask for help. Listen for answers. Pray for others. Ask to be shown how to be of service. Offer your thanks. Find a community that supports your personal faith. Live your life in accordance with how you think your God wants you to live. Surrender. When you don't have the answers, know that perhaps Someone else does. See your Higher Power speak, act and work through others in your life. Find answers to life's big questions that make sense to you, even if you don't fully understand the how or the why. Create your own version of heaven.

Divorce your own personal spirituality from religion. Even if you consider yourself a religious person and are involved with an organized group, find your own faith that resonates with you independent of your groups. How does your faith inform your day? Your decisions? Your actions? Would your God be proud of you? What would your Higher Power say about you?

When things are not going right in your life and you feel discouraged, choose to find a Friend, Counselor, Mentor and Guide in your own personal Creation. Western Psychology for most of its history has been shamefully negligent in allowing for the possibility that the best personal psychology of all is found in one's connection with a Source greater than themselves. Consider the possibility that you are here for a reason, that you are destined for greatness and that you are deeply, deeply, deeply loved. Consider the possibility that you can simply choose to believe just simply to feel better. Why wouldn't you?

PRINCIPLE 9

Still Your Mind

*"All of humanity's problems stem from man's inability
to sit quietly in a room alone." – Blaise Pascal*

Research is increasingly proving what Eastern gurus have known all along; that a quiet mind leads to a serene heart. Meditation and relaxation exercises have been shown to be as effective as psycho-pharmaceutical drugs in treating depression, anxiety and other ailments. Of course, taking a pill is much more suited to the American quick-fix mentality, but I will suggest a simple, non-intimidating and hopefully effective means to still your monkey mind.

Every single person I have worked with or met who has dabbled in meditation has stated that they are not very good at meditation, that their mind won't stop racing, so of course they are quick to drop the practice like a bad date. No one is good at meditation and quieting the mind when they start. That is the point. That is why we all need it.

So before you start a practice, know that you are going to feel like you are doing it wrong, that you just aren't suited to meditation, that your mind is racing. Even though you don't feel like you are getting the benefits right away, you are learning to train your mind. Just as you wouldn't bemoan the fact that you didn't have huge muscles after only a couple days of lifting weights or be ready for a marathon after a week of running, trust that mind training takes practice and dedication as well.

The most important factor to consider when beginning a mind-stilling program is to choose a format that is realistic to incorporate into your day. Some of the advanced meditation programs advocate two hour long sessions. I recognize that for most of us, we simply don't have that luxury. And the benefits of relaxation training are still available even if we incorporate one or two short sessions per day. The key is to choose something that is habit forming. So ultimately, just as we brush our teeth, shower, check email, eat, get dressed and all of the other routines of life, we take a moment to still our mind.

So how does one still the mind? To start with just simply look at your day and carve out one 5 minute period where you can be alone and quiet. It can be in your bedroom, your car, your bathroom, your office or anywhere where you will be un-interrupted. Look at a clock and tell yourself you are going to be still for the next 5 minutes. Ask yourself to save your thoughts for later. Now I guarantee that many, many thoughts will arise, but your goal in the first few attempts is to simply acknowledge the thoughts and allow them to pass by. Visualize a sailboat or a cloud floating away with them.

Many people like to focus on their breath, concentrating on inhaling or exhaling. Other options include choosing a mantra to repeat internally; e.g. I am at Peace, All is well, I am Love, or anything that resonates with you. Ultimately, it does not matter how you choose to be still, just do it day in and day out and you will begin to want to return to your quiet, safe place.

If you are really struggling after many attempts at solo stillness, you can also find many guided meditations to download onto your mobile device. I-Tunes University offers many free downloads and is a great resource to try out different forms of guided meditation. There are also many great apps that offer similar guidance.

Learning to still your mind is the ultimate act of self-love. By quieting the mind and allowing ones thoughts to dissipate, it opens the channels for new energy to come into your life. With a full, busy and racing mind, there is no room for you to receive guidance from forces more powerful than yourself. It is in the stillness that your greater good becomes available to you.

Principle 10

Remove Toxic Energy

"Everything is energy and that's all there is to it. Match the frequency of the reality you want and you cannot help but get that reality. It can be no other way. This is not philosophy. This is physics." -Albert Einstein

We live in an energetic universe. What does that mean? It means that we receive feelings, attitudes, judgments, creativity, emotions, sustenance, and information from every single thing we encounter. People, places, things; they all bring to us their level of consciousness and impact us energetically.

What does it mean to be impacted energetically? Just think about how you feel when you walk out of a movie theatre. Your body, mind and spirit have a 'felt sense' of what you have just experienced on the screen. If it was an uplifting story, you might feel a bit lighter, joyful and loving. If the movie was disturbing, you might feel anxious, uneasy or weary. The movie experience is just a magnified example of what we all experience each and every moment of our lives. There is nothing in the world that does not carry with it energy. This energy affects each and every cell in your body. You are impacted, good or bad, by every animate and inanimate thing in the universe.

Take responsibility for the energy you allow into your life. You get to decide what you allow into your space. Food, drinks, television, emails, books, people, websites, i-phone apps, clothes, furnishings, music, pets, and more: everything in your world affects you on an energetic level. The good news is that you have the choice over much of what you allow into your energy field.

"Power versus Force", a marvelous book by David Hawkins provides incredible scientific examples of just how we are all impacted by the cosmic energy contained in everyday items. He uses the famous arm strength test to demonstrate how certain thoughts, feelings, books, food and other miscellaneous items calibrate as either positive or negative energy. For instance, if you held a banana, apple or a picture of the Dalai Lama, and someone tried to push your arms down, your muscles would stay strong and you would be able to withstand their force. Conversely, if you held candy, cigarettes or a picture of Hitler, your muscles would be weaker and someone could easily push your arm down. If you don't believe it, find a friend and give it a try.

Another fun energy experiment is to buy some flowers and divide them in half and place into two vases. On one vase write the words, "Love, Peace, Joy, Happiness, Light" or other similar words and tape it to the vase. The second vase should contain words like, "Hate, Evil, Death, Devil, Darkness." I have yet to conduct this experiment where the flowers in vase one were noticeably healthier, longer-living and vital. Energy – words, thoughts, emotion - matters.

Here are some of the main energy vampires; items that drain your energy and are toxic to your system: 24 hour television news, drugs and alcohol, processed unhealthy foods, negative people, violent shows or movies, toxic people, and negative thoughts. Keep this concept in mind as you make all of the tiny little choices that shape our day. Do you wake up and turn on the television to hear about the latest shootings in town, or do you pick up spiritual literature? Do you grab a bag of processed potato chips or an apple? Do you have a cocktail after work or sit down with a soul-nourishing book and cup of tea?

Every single little choice you make ultimately impacts your mood and your well-being. The good news is that for the vast majority of things we encounter, we have the luxury of choosing whether or not we want to allow them into our energy field. Choose your energy wisely. Think about what you would want to expose to an innocent newborn child and then treat yourself with the same love and compassion.

There are times, however, when we can't avoid certain situations that carry with them negative energy or we are forced to be around a toxic person. In these situations create in your mind's eye an energy shield to protect you from the negativity. A visual that works is envisioning a bright light surrounding your body much like bubble. Mentally picture this bubble deflecting the negative energy back into the universe.

Choose positive energy to light up your life. Whether it be a flower in your kitchen, soothing music, regular massages, loving people, sunshine, healthy foods, uplifting books, loving pets, beautiful jewelry, nourishing artwork or angels; let the good stuff in. Take responsibility for your environment. But know you don't have to become a slave to perfection. Nobody can make it through a day without at least some less then healthy energetic substances. So of course an occasional bout of negativity, junk-food, cocktail or violent show won't destroy your overall well-being, but it is wise to be mindful of the notion that everything carries its own positive or negative energy field.

You do not have to be a victim of the myriad environmental toxins and energy vampires lurking in the midst. Love yourself enough to surround yourself with love. Take responsibility for the energy you allow into your vibration.

PRINCIPLE 11

Love Is An Action Verb

"Love is a verb. It is an action requiring your involvement
and active participation. You cannot sit back and expect
that the world will serve it to you." – Stephen Covey

Love is not just a feeling. Love is an action verb. Love is
what you do, not just what you say or what you feel. Love
is demonstrated through specific concrete behaviors that are
tangible and real.

Romantic love is one of the most complicated endeavors of
all human behavior. We have all at one time or another been
caught up in the drama of a love affair. Do I love him? Does
she love me? Is he the "one?" How do we know if we are really
in love and connecting romantically with the perfect partner
for us? Look at your actions, not your feelings.

Our feelings often get us in trouble in romantic relationships. **We confuse lust with love, neediness for worthiness and drama with passion.** To determine whether or not you are really "in love" with someone, ask yourself the following questions:

> *Do I want to spend my time with this person?*
> *Do I feel motivated to demonstrate loving, caring actions towards this person?*
> *Do I want to create a life with this person?*
> *Do I want wonderful things to happen to this person?*

Conversely, if you are wondering if your significant other really does in fact love you, despite his pleas that he does, ask yourself these questions:

> *How does she show me she loves me?*
> *What does he do each day that demonstrates to me that he cares about my well-being?*
> *Is she acting in a manner that shows me she wants to create a life with me?*

For instance, a man who proclaims his undying love and devotion to his mistress, but still lives at home with his wife, is not demonstrating love. A woman who verbally attacks her boyfriend continuously is not being love. A partner who continually prefers to spend time with others instead of his lover is not showing love.

Look at a person's actions, not what they are saying. Loving words certainly can be nice to hear, and when matched by their actions, can be beautiful; but words alone mean little. Make your romantic decisions in your life by a person's actions, not their statements. And just because someone tells you they won't repeat a certain unhealthy behavior again, don't believe them. Wait for their actions to speak for them. Love yourself enough to choose a partner who doesn't just tell you she loves you, but shows you that love.

Principle 12

Do the Next Right Thing

"A successful person places more attention on doing the right thing rather than doing things right." – Peter Drucker

Recovery groups encourage their adherents that when in doubt, to simply 'do the next right thing.' What does that mean exactly? Essentially, it is breaking down your day into very specific moments and with each given choice during the day to simply choose to do the next right thing. Most of us don't know what the "best" or "right" course of action for our overall life plan entails, but we can certainly make the smaller decisions that make up our day to the best of our ability. We can choose to simply do the next right thing and then take the necessary action inherent in that decision.

The phone rings. It is someone trying to collect money you owe him. What is the right action? Answer the phone. Make a plan for re-payment. Your kitchen is a mess. Clean it. Your dog needs to go outside. Take him. Your girlfriend has seemed sad and down. Bring her roses. The basement is flooding. Call a plumber. You are hungry. Eat. You are tired. Sleep. You need comfort. Ask for it.

This principle works for the big things in life as well as the small things. Breaking down the big things in your life into small manageable tasks of simply doing the next right thing and taking the next right action allows you to not feel overwhelmed by the perceived enormity of your situation. You lost your job. Breathe. Seek solace in friends. Make some calls. Network. Continue to do the next right thing and these small actions will eventually lead to a positive outcome.

Every action we take makes a difference in the overall course of our life. Choose each action wisely. Our life is simply a compilation of the small decisions we make in each moment. A lifetime of 'doing the next right thing' will lead to a lifetime of joy, contentment and inner peace.

Principle 13

Set Intentions, not Goals

"All that counts in life is intention." - Andre Boccelli

Some of the best advice I ever received from a mentor was, *"you can't plan an inspired life."* Before I received that guidance from a trusted advisor, I was consumed with goal-writing and checking off the goals on my list much like a grocery list. What I didn't realize, however, was that in being so specific, rigid and defined, I was actually narrowing down the options that the Universe had for me. My little ego mind cannot possibly conceive of the vast greatness that is available to me if I simply get out of my way. Therefore, I shifted from 'goal-writing' to 'intention setting'.

An "inspired" life is one in which an individual feels a sense of joy, ecstasy, love and passion in their activities.

Inspired literally means to be living 'in spirit'. There is a deep connection with something larger than their limited sense of self. To live a truly inspired life, I needed to stop setting goals that my limited ego self could conceive, and instead tap into my intuition. I am than able to get inspired to create and take actions that I might not have ever dreamed of by simply following my inner guidance and paying attention to the many guideposts life provides.

When one is caught up in goal-setting and achievement-focused orientation, there is a tendency to lose the joy of the process and get too focused on outcomes. How many people have we all witnessed who seemed consumed to achieve more and may even succeed, but are unhappy and joyless? Think of all of the professional or collegiate athletes who admit that in their goal-focused quest to achieve they lost the joy of the game. Or the multi-millionaire corporate scion who admits to having awful familial relationships?

Writing life goals can consume us negatively in a similar fashion if we are narrow-minded and fail to allow for input from the Universe. If your goal is to become Vice President of the bank you work for and you get laid off, then what? A goal-focused mind-set would be to feel like a failure. It is possible; however, that the layoff occurred so your greatness could emerge and you could be hired for a hirer paying joy at a higher level at another bank or go after the "dream job" you have been afraid to really pursue. Or perhaps your goal is to get engaged and your boyfriend breaks up with you. Then what? As the old saying goes, "Man's rejection is often God's protection." Perhaps there is a relationship far greater than you can imagine waiting for you. While your "goal" may be shattered, having the mind-set of living an "inspired" life allows you the possibility to view the lack of achievement of specific pre-determined goals as the Universe's way of saying, "nope, I've got different and better plans for your life."

What does it mean to set intentions? Intentions convey a broader spectrum of possibilities than goals. Intentions allow for the unexpected. Intentions allow for guidance from something beyond your finite mind. Intentions involve feelings. An example of intention vs. goal is as follows: Instead of setting the goal of losing 25 lbs., create an intention to have a healthy beautiful vibrant body that fits into your favorite pair of new jeans. Visualize your intention to work towards manifestation. Doesn't that feel better than simply writing down, "I will lose 25 lbs?"

When you think about what intentions you want to set for your life, think about how you want to feel. What is the feeling you are going after when you tell yourself that in X number of years you want to have this much money, this many kids, etc.? Allow yourself to revel in how you imagine you might feel once you have achieved that benchmark. And then set your intention.

Intentions allow for possibilities. If for some reason, the goal you set for yourself doesn't pan out as plan, you revert back into the mind-set of the feeling you were going after and craft new intentions that will likely bring about the same outcome. Therefore you are not failing when things don't go as planned, but rather you need to find a different avenue to get to the feeling state you are after.

If things aren't flowing you are moving in the wrong direction. If you are pursuing something relentlessly and nothing seems to go your way, consider the possibility that the Universe has different plans for you. Yes, we have all heard the story about the authors who got published after their 200th try and the message seems to be, never ever, ever, ever, ever give up. But what I believe these successful people don't share with you is the small bits of validation they received along the way that demonstrated they were headed in the right direction. Yes, continue to pursue your dreams despite rejection; but also take time to listen and to make sure you are not setting yourself up for a life of paddling upstream. One may have a dream of becoming a professional tennis player, but if you simply don't have the talent, no amount of persistence is going to change that reality. Find what you are good at and set intentions around your strengths.

Forget goals. Set intentions. Intentions are based on the idea that you cannot plan a life of inspiration, intuition and creativity. Intentions allow for change. Goals are often too rigid. Perhaps it is just a semantic trick, but replacing intentions with goals is an excellent method to move forward in the direction of your dreams without getting discouraged when things don't go exactly as you planned. Sometimes Life has better ideas than you do.

Principle 14

Read, Read, Read!!

"We need to read to know we are not alone." – *C.S. Lewis*
"Read, read, read." - *William Faulkner*

The worst advice I received was from an Assistant Professor of Psychology who told his students to never read pop psychology or self-help books. Not much later I came across my first self-help book by the father of motivation Wayne Dyer. While I thought about what the professor said and originally intended to follow his advice, I ultimately disobeyed.

I was struck by how practical the information in Wayne Dyer's book was and how unhelpful the academic journals and books I had been reading were. While I prided myself on my academic credentials, I had to admit that the people with the highest degrees and the highest so-called intelligence didn't necessarily seem to have it all together. And as I thought of the overweight, melancholy, single assistant professor and juxtaposed his life against the vibrant, full and loving life Wayne Dyer (who incidentally has a Ph.D. but determined to write practical books for laypeople) and other pop psychology authors were living, I realized that perhaps academic psychology didn't have all the answers. Consequently, while not abandoning the academic journals, I gave myself the freedom to read whatever I wanted.

Nearly all successful peak performers in a wide variety of disciples have acknowledged that their key to success was a voracious appetite for reading. I was blessed with a very early love of reading and devoured everything at an early age. Whether it is fiction, non-fiction, biography, newspaper, journals, Twitter feeds and more, READ.

Read to learn. Whether it is learning how to ski, to cook, or learning to control your emotions, there is an amazing power at tapping into books to grow. Through books we are given the opportunity to compare our inner lives with the lives of others. In most of life we compare our insides to other people's outsides; assuming everybody else has it together. Or in this day and age, we often compare our insides to other people's glamorous Instagram and Facebook posts, again assuming their lives are perfect.

Books allow us to glimpse the actual internal lives of others. In reality, we are all a combination of beauty and brokenness and it is in hearing someone else's story and how they overcame obstacles that you can truly grow. Read self-help books, spiritual books, biographies, comic books, fiction, non-fiction, classics, erotica, travel, cookbooks. The genre does not matter. Simply read. And learn. And put into practice anything useful.

PRINCIPLE 15

Practice Gratitude

"Gratitude opens the door to...the power, the wisdom, the creativity of the universe. You open the door through gratitude". – Deepak Chopra

Gratitude is a state of appreciation for your world exactly as it is in this moment. It is the release of striving for things to be as they are not. The ability to cultivate gratitude and to live in a state of thankfulness for what you have is the key to optimal emotional wellness.

What is gratitude exactly? It is the ability to really feel that the universe is conspiring for your greater good and to offer your deep thanks for Its wisdom. Gratitude is to know that in all things lays a seed of perfection, growth or opportunity. Gratitude is the belief that you are not given more than you can handle. Gratitude is being thankful for the simple things in life. Gratitude is joy in living and appreciation for the beauty in the simplest of moments. Gratitude is thankfulness in action. Gratitude is respect for the inherent perfection in life. Gratitude is love combined with humility.

Like anything, gratitude must to be put into practice for its benefits to be realized. Flex your gratitude muscle. To do this, create a gratitude ritual that resonates with you. Some ideas to incorporate into a ritual in your life include; keeping a gratitude journal (list 5 things a day to be grateful for), verbally affirm each morning what you are grateful for, show your gratitude by an act of service at least once a day, or simply take 5 minutes to do a gratitude meditation.

Whatever means you have for consciously inviting the idea of gratitude into your life; make it a habit. For some of us, gratitude is a more natural state of being. For others, it is a muscle we need to flex and strengthen. But for all of us, regardless of our current level of gratitude, consciously creating gratitude moments in our life will only serve to enhance our emotional well-being.

As Nietzsche stated, *"If the only prayer you ever uttered was thank you; that would suffice."* Thank you.

Principle 16

Progress, Not Perfection

"Understanding the difference between healthy
striving and perfectionism is critical to laying
down the shield and picking up your life.
Research shows that perfectionism hampers success. In fact, it's
often the path to depression, anxiety, addiction, and life paralysis."
– Brené Brown

The paradox of life is that we are all inherently perfect and deeply flawed. Our essence is wholeness but our humanness is brokenness. Our hearts are often pure but our heads are clouded. We are not meant to be perfect here on this plane of existence. We are meant to grow and learn from our mistakes.

The only useful question to ask of yourself when determining your progress on any emotional, personal or spiritual path is:

Am I a better me today than I was yesterday? Am I growing in the right direction? Am I improving?

The co-founder of AA, Bill Wilson, coined this notion of progress rather than perfection. He wisely realized how one's perfection can be their greatest character defect and can sabotage their recovery. Expecting perfection from your-self is inherently flawed as there is no universal concept of perfection and no universal rule of what constitutes perfect living. The best any of us can do is to strive to align our beliefs and values with our actions. And of course we will fail at times. But are we making progress? That is the only appropriate question to ask of oneself.

How do you measure progress? To me, the biggest measure of progress is simply whether or not you are better today than you were yesterday. Apathy, indifference and the inability to strive to be the best you can be are truly the only signs of someone who is not progressing. Are you taking risks? Are you striving? Are you trying to be the best version of yourself? As Brene Brown, the esteemed "Shame" researcher shares, "Are you in the arena? Are you daring greatly?"

Let go of the unrealistic idea of perfection. See to it that you are simply progressing, and your life will slowly unfold beautifully and imperfectly.

Principle 17

The Power of Journaling

"What a comfort is this journal I tell myself to myself and throw the burden on my book and feel relieved." -Anne Lister

Journaling is a powerful method of capturing ones progress in life; emotionally, professionally, spiritually, relationally and more. We are able to view through our own written words our strengths, our fears, and ultimately; with the clarity of time; our progress.

Create the habit of journaling. Release any pre-conceived notions of what a journal is supposed to be. In particular, let go of the idea that a journal has to chronicle every detail of your life, that you must write in it every day, and that you must have perfect grammar and prose. Your journal is simply your record of your unconscious. There are no rules to journaling.

Journaling, whether it is writing with a pen and notebook or typing, allows you to access a part of your brain that is often dormant. Journaling allows you to tap into your subconscious and tap into the right-side of your brain. The right side of our brain is the intuitive, romantic, artistic and creative aspect of our being. The left side is often the part of the brain that is most active throughout the course of our day; the logical, linear, rational aspect of our self. The mere act of writing or typing, particularly as we censor that voice in our head that tells us how to do it, what to write, how to make it sound good, etc., opens us up to the part of our being that is driven by our subconscious, intuitive and Higher Self.

Journaling can also act as the most efficient and inexpensive therapist around. Often we all simply need to release our emotions, our story, our anger, our fears, our heartache, and journaling provides that release. Re-reading your journal entry, particularly out loud, will further allow for healthy processing of these turbulent emotions.

Create a beautiful journal ritual that works with your own life. Let you express you the way only you know how to do. Write. Draw. Question. Dialog. Vent. Love. Pray. Journal. Your Highest Self will thank you. The part of you that wants to be heard but is suppressed will thank you. Journaling opens the door to meet the very best part of your being.

PRINCIPLE 18

Feel Your Feelings

*"Mankind are governed more by their feelings
than by reason." – Samuel Adams*

Your feelings are like toddlers that are tugging on their parents' pant-legs, just begging to be acknowledged. As much as I believe in and espouse the importance of positive thinking, I do recognize that lost in all of the hub-bub of thinking positive is the importance of actually acknowledging and respecting the very real feelings we do have, including the negative ones. Just because we have a negative feelings about something doesn't mean we are sabotaging our emotional well-being. In fact, talking ourselves out of feeling the feeling is often what gets us into more trouble emotionally.

The trick is to not get caught and stuck in our negative feelings. There is a method to allow our feelings their space, but to not allow them to occupy. **The steps to take in order to recognize our feelings in a healthy way are: 1) Awareness 2) Acceptance 3) Experience and 4) Release.**

Awareness is simply consciously acknowledging that a feeling is present. Yes, I am jealous of my brother. Yes, I am mad at my boss. Yes, I am annoyed at my whining toddler. Yes, I do feel tired. Saying yes and giving ourselves permission to have an emotion is the first step in our ability to release it in a healthy way. Denying the feeling and quickly shifting into a positive affirmation or attempt at gratitude will ultimately suppress the feeling, causing it to resurface in a different medium. Consciously acknowledge the feeling, even if it is a dark thought.

The second step is to really accept it. Acceptance doesn't mean that you are allowing the feeling to become a permanent guest in your brain. It simply means that you accept that for whatever reason you are having the particular negative thought. You don't need to judge the feeling. Just step outside and observe your emotional state, and say, 'wow, how interesting. I'm really upset about _____'. Be a witness to the feeling and accept that you are in a particular mood. The important thing about acceptance is to not confuse it with understanding. You do not need to understand something to accept it. So often when we feel a certain way, there is an obsessive quest to figure out why. If you are teary, you quickly shift to a mental list of things that you might be sad about. Accept that sometimes you are just sad and teary because you are. There might not be anything in particular that needs to change at that moment. Allow the feeling. Accept the feeling. Don't analyze the feeling.

Once you have acknowledged and accepted the feeling, the third step is to actually experience the feelings. You might be thinking, "What? This is a self-help book! Why in the world would I want to consciously choose to feel a bad feeling?" You want to feel your feelings so that they don't get buried in your unconscious and then resurface in terrible ways, such as addictions, bursts of anger, physical disease and more. Often our fear of diving into the feeling is actually more painful than the feeling itself.

The trick is to feel the feeling for a very limited time period. During this time, you will recognize that it is not as painful as you thought, or you can console yourself that it will be over very soon. So how do you consciously experience the feeling? Set aside a very short amount of time where you will be undisturbed, about five minutes or even less depending on the intensity of the emotion. Set a timer. Take a few deep breaths and then consciously bring to your mind the upset feeling. Sit and really, really FEEL the feeling. Let whatever emotions or behaviors arise without any judgment. Cry. Scream. Sob. Laugh. Just feel. But then stop after five minutes. Your feeling time is over.

The final step is to release the feeling. To release the feeling you need to create a very specific and concrete visual image that resonates with you and that represents an actual physical release of the emotion. Some ideas include; imagine the feeling word actually burning and being disintegrated into smoke, pack up the feeling in a hot air balloon and send it off, throw the feeling like a snowball and watch it melt in the sun, toss the feeling in a river and see it get absorbed by the flowing water, watch it go down the drain, etc. Get creative. Find a visual image that works for you and then mentally release the feeling. You can internally repeat a closing mantra such as, 'thanks for sharing. I don't need you anymore. I am free.' The key is to do the exact same thing every time you want to release a feeling. The repetition of the specific release mechanism is what will trigger your unconscious to mentally release the mental anguish. Remember, however, that you must have completed the first three steps before releasing.

Awareness. Acceptance. Experience. Release. This is your formula for processing your feelings in an emotionally mature and healthy way. The whole process should take you 10 minutes of less. Keep it simple.

PRINCIPLE 19

Choose Happiness Over Rightness

"Do you prefer that you be right or happy?" – *A Course in Miracles*

This wonderful question originally appeared in *A Course in Miracles*, a marvelous psycho-spiritual self-teaching program that incidentally started me on my spiritual path. The text poses the profound question regarding whether it is more valuable for your ego to feel satisfied that your perspective is correct, or is it more important that your Higher Self concedes to the deeper truth and knowingness that it is in fact more important to be happy.

Is it more important for you to be happy or right? Is it usually more important for you to be right than to be at peace? Would you rather get the last word in than feel serene? Is your self-esteem tied to being right? Are you convinced that you have all the answers? If you answered yes to any of those questions, you are not on the highest path of emotional growth.

Choosing happiness over 'rightness' is one means of obtaining serenity and peace-of-mind. That does not mean that you need to neglect your needs or allow people to walk all over you. It simply means that you consciously decide to let certain things go. It means that you decide some things in life are simply not worth arguing about.

Detaching is a crucial concept when considering letting go of the egoic need to be right. To detach means to "separate, to disengage." When you are in an argument with someone simply disengage. You don't need to proclaim your rightness. You simply let go of your attachment to your viewpoint.

A very simple phrase has been known to ease many a conflict. Simply state, "You may be right." Offer a smile. Detach with love. And ask your Higher Self if it feels better or worse? If you are wholly attached to the ego, you might actually feel worse right away. But the long term benefits of choosing to be happy over being right far outweighs the discomfort of long-term relationship strife caused by the neurotic egoic need to be right. Choose happiness.

PRINCIPLE 20

Action is More Important than Understanding

"In Zen, actions speak louder than words. Doing is more important than knowing, and knowledge which cannot be translated into actions is of little worth." –Thick Thien-An

A popular quote from the Big Book (the basic text of Alcoholics Anonymous) states, "Self-knowledge availed us nothing." This notion that a life run on self-knowledge alone is ultimately self-defeating is a key concept to understand when trying to make changes in our life.

Popular culture and popular psychology allows us to believe in the myth that we must understand why we are a certain way before we can change it. That is simply not true. Self-understanding may or may not be a by-product of transformative change, but it is not a necessary ingredient. To change, just simply change. Ok, that sounds simple, but a first step in changing any unwelcome behavior is to actually believe it is possible. It is important to believe change is achievable with as little baggage surrounding it as possible. Therefore, you do not have to know why you eat, drink, gamble or have sex compulsively before you begin to change the behavior.

A necessary ingredient of change when dealing with a seemingly stubborn, persistent or addictive pattern of behavior is to cultivate an attitude of surrender. What we resist persists. Therefore, accept and then surrender the behavior. Acknowledge that it is there, and then consciously surrender the behavior to something outside of yourself. Say, 'I have no control over this behavior, but I am willing to give it away to the Universe. I no longer need it.' Then ask for help from whatever greater Power you can conceive of. It is that simple.

Let go of the societal messages that tell us we need to discover our inner child, heal every single relationship, forgive everyone and everything, and understand exactly why we are the way we are before we can heal. Self-knowledge can be an interesting journey and often ultimately does allow someone to heal, but often it is not necessary to bring about positive change in your life. Personal wellness is a lot simpler and easier than many would have us believe. You can have a great life simply because you decide to.

PRINCIPLE 21

Humility is Absolutely Necessary

"Humility is the solid foundation of all the virtues"
- Confucius

Humility is defined as "a modest view of one's own importance." Some may think that this is contrary to the messages of self-love and acceptance I have been espousing. Humility is important because it is a form of healthy detachment from obsessing over your-self. **Humility is not about thinking less of your-self; rather it is thinking of your-self less.** That is why my self-help book is short, concise and practical. I do not believe anyone needs to spend countless hours on self-improvement (even though I am guilty of just such behavior – professional hazard☺). Learn a few practical tools to stay sane and then get out of your own way and get busy living and serving.

Humility allows you to do just that. Humility is the cornerstone of healthy self-acceptance and a willingness to be there for others. An attitude of humility means that we don't think we are greater than others or that our problems are greater than others. A common misconception is when someone thinks they are being humble by stating how awful their life is, how they are depressed and miserable. That is not humility. It is self-pity.

A humble person is joyful just simply to be alive. He or she accepts his lot in life with ease and grace. A humble person takes actions towards his goals but doesn't remain attached to the outcome. Humility means being comfortable just as one is. Invite humility into your life.

Conclusion

In summary:

Thoughts matter. Choose good ones.
To get self-esteem, do esteemable things.
Accept that most people are difficult.
Act as if you are happy.
Be your own best friend.
Denial is ok sometimes.
Find a faith that works.
Still your mind. Cultivate silence.
Remove toxic energy.
Remember that love is an action verb. Be love.
Do the next right thing.
Set intentions, not goals.
Read.
Practice gratitude.
Aim for progress, not perfection.

Journal.
Accept and feel your feelings.
Decide happiness is more important than being right.
Know that action is more important than understanding.
Be humble.

Emotional wellness is not as complicated as one would have you believe. We are not victims of our past or any mental state that we may have been told we might have. As much as the de-stigmatization of mental illness has been positive in some respects, I do believe it carried with it new negative consequences. Often people carry around their mental health labels like a proud wounded soldier, hiding behind a diagnosis so they don't have to live a great life. With that said, seek professional treatment immediately if you are suffering from severely debilitating mental health issues. Professionals can and will help you get to a stable point so you can then incorporate these practical principles into your life.

Yes, some people do suffer from severe emotional and other pathological problems and need medication and intense treatment. But for the vast majority of us, we are healthy, sane beings when we decide we are. We are not victims of our past or products of an unhealthy society. We are human beings with free will. We can choose joy.

My hope is that this little personal growth book can be a simple tool in helping you release any negative patterns that may have developed and can be a resource to return to if you feel stuck. You have the power to create the life of your dreams. You have the power to enjoy the passage of time. You get to decide if this life is one of joy or one of fear. Choose joy.

Appendix

Below please find some worksheets that I have used with clients as part of an 8 week *Personal Empowerment Program (PEP)*. The goal with these activities and this program is different than traditional psychotherapy. Rather than minimizing or reducing mental illness, this program and series of worksheets aim to optimize well-being. Based on the principles of positive psychology, spiritual truths and much of the material in this little book, these exercises should help you in your journey towards cultivating a joy-filled life.

PERSONAL EMPOWERMENT PROGRAM – WEEK 1:

Paying attention to our self-talk is very important for our mental health. Making the decision that internal verbal abuse is not acceptable behavior is the first step towards finding inner peace and freedom from emotional pain. Finding the balance between observing our negative thoughts and engaging with the thoughts is essential for our emotional healing. The healthiest way to move through an emotion effectively is to surrender completely to the emotion when it comes over you. Resign to the feeling for a short period of time, no longer than 90 seconds. Let yourself FEEL the emotion. Just like children, emotions heal when they are heard and validated. Once you allow yourself to feel the emotion that came from the self-talk, use one of these strategies to replace the negative emotional activities and thoughts:

1) Create a mantra and repeat internally. Examples of mantra's –"I am at peace. All is well in my world. I love and accept myself. Joy overflows in my life. I am loving. I am happy, joyous and free."

    MyMantra:_____

    _____

    _____

    _____

    _____

Remember, it is the action of the mantra that works, not your conscious belief. Just do it, even if at the time you don't believe it.

2) Think about something that brings me terrific joy. E.g. Skiing, being with your dog, cooking, Hawaiian vacation, Disneyland vacation with kids, scuba diving, singing...

My JOY thoughts:_____

_____

_____

_____

_____

3) Think about a favorite song lyric, poem, prayer or something else short, concise and positive that is easy to remember and has a catchy cadence. e.g. The Serenity Prayer, "Don't Worry Be Happy", "It's Going to Be a Bright Sunshiny Day."

My Song/Prayer/Poem:_____

_____

_____

_____

_____

4) Think about something that you would like to do in the future that excites you. E.g. Climb a mountain, write a book, take the family on a Mexican vacation, run a marathon.

My future goals/plans that excite me and bring me joy:

_____

_____

_____

_____

Remember that WHAT YOU THINK ABOUT EXPANDS. You have a choice over the content of your thoughts. You don't always get to choose the first thought that shows up, but it is your choice as to whether or not you want to follow a negative train of thought. Choose joyful thoughts. Your joyful thoughts will eventually lead to more joyful and peaceful emotions.

Exercise for people dealing with a major loss, transition of life crisis that deserves some focus and attention, e.g. divorce, death, etc.

EMOTION FEELING TIME: Allow yourself a 10 or 15 time period each day to indulge in your feelings of sadness, anger, pain and fear. Choose a specific time of day to let yourself really FEEL the emotions. Cry, yell, scream, etc. During the day when these emotions come up, tell yourself to wait until your allotted "Emotion Feeling" time.

PERSONAL EMPOWERMENT PROGRAM – WEEK 2:

Wellness Inventory

On a scale from 1 to 5 (1 being 'not at all' to 5 being 'all the time'), score how well you are doing in each of these areas of your life.

Social Wellness

____I connect with family and friends on a consistent basis

____I communicate honestly and respectfully when seeking to resolve conflicts

____I maintain a diverse and strong support system.

____I am able to give and receive in relationships.

____I give of my talents or economic resources to better the world around me.

Physical Wellness

____I exercise 3 or more times per week for at least 30 minutes.

____I eat a nutritious diet on a daily basis.

____I maintain regular preventive doctor appointments.

____I take proactive steps to avoid illness, injury and disease.

____I manage stress by doing activities that promote relaxation.

Intellectual Wellness

____I view learning as a lifelong process and can change my views.

____I take risks and learn from my mistakes.

____I seek out ways to challenge and stretch my mind.

_____In conversations, I can listen to ideas different from my own and constantly re-examine my perspectives.

_____I appreciate the creative arts.

Emotional Wellness

_____I accept and appreciate my worth as a human being.

_____I express my feelings in a healthy manner.

_____I recognize that I create my own feelings and take responsibility for them.

____I avoid blaming other people or situations for my feelings and behavior.

____I can own my limitations and cope effectively with the ups and downs of life.

Spiritual Wellness

____ I usually demonstrate consistency between my values and how I live my life.

____I have a deep appreciation for the gift of life.

____I constantly seek ways to deepen and grow spiritually.

____I appreciate the uniqueness of all individuals and experience a sense of inter-connectedness with all/most people.

____I have a "WHY" I live for.

For any areas you scored a 1 or 2, please write down specific action items you will complete to raise your score to work towards optimal emotional wellness.

Social Wellness

Physical Wellness

Intellectual Wellness

Emotional Wellness

Spiritual Wellness

PERSONAL EMPOWERMENT PROGRAM – WEEK 3:

FORGIVENESS EXERCISE – "ANGRY LOVE LETTER"

Forgiveness is for you, not for the person that needs to be forgiven. Think of someone in your life who you need to forgive. Forgiveness does not mean you are letting them off the hook or condoning abusive behavior. It simply means that you are deciding to no longer allow your unforgiving feelings to have a negative impact in your life.

Exercise: Write an "Angry Love Letter". This letter is NOT to be sent. This is only for your personal healing process. The content of the letter should be as follows:

- Dear _____,
- Write down every bad, terrible, cruel, mean, unloving person thing that this person did for you. This is your opportunity to release all of your negative emotions. Curse, vent, YELL to the paper. Let it all out.
- Take responsibility for any part you may have had in the conflict. This is your opportunity to reflect on your own part in the conflict. Outline in writing the errors in your ways.
- Indicate anything that you may still like or even love about them (even if it is as small as 'they are nice to their dog'.) Find whatever you can to love about this person.
- When finished with the letter, read it out load.
- Do not send the letter!
- Discard the letter in a symbolic manner- burn, shred, etc.

Letter:

Dear _____,

_____
_____
_____
_____
_____
_____
_____
_____
_____
_____
_____
_____
_____
_____
_____
_____
_____
_____
_____
_____
_____
_____

In forgiveness,

_____

Finally, complete and sign this written statement of forgiveness. When you find yourself ruminating or thinking negatively about the person, bring your attention, either internally or literally, to this statement below.

I, _____, decide right now on _____(date), to forgive _____. I no longer need to carry around anger, hurt and pain. I am free.

*This worksheet should be photo-copied and completed as many times and for as many situations as necessary.

PERSONAL EMPOWERMENT PROGRAM – WEEK 4:

PROCESSING FEELINGS WORKSHEET

Most psychological problems are a result of suppressing feelings. This worksheet is designed to be completed whenever there is a strong feeling that is causing emotional turmoil. Usually our instinct is to deny, bury, rationalize or pretend the feeling isn't there. That just creates long term problems.

There is a method to allow our feelings their space, but to not allow them to occupy. The steps to take in order to recognize our feelings in a healthy way are: 1) Awareness 2) Acceptance 3) Experience and 4) Release. When we have taken ourselves through these feelings steps we are no longer burdened by the thoughts and are much less likely to develop a mental illness.

1. **Awareness: Describe the feeling in as much detail as possible.**

e.g. I feel sad and angry that I didn't get the job I applied for. I feel like a failure and that nothing is working out in my life. I feel like a loser. My stomach hurts.

_____

_____

_____

_____

2. <u>Acceptance:</u> Consciously accept and invite the feeling in.

e.g. I accept this sadness right now. I am disappointed they didn't hire me. I accept that I am taking this personally and feeling so low. I accept that I feel this pain physically.

_____

_____

_____

_____

3. <u>Experience:</u> Set a timer for 5 minutes. Sit with the feeling in silence for that amount of time. Allow yourself to feel. Cry. Yell. Do whatever feels natural. Give in to the feeling without pushing it away. Finally, jot down any notes about what came up for you.

e.g. Wow, I'm surprised I cried that hard. That felt good. I think I am also angry too that they didn't see how perfect I was for the job. My stomach feels less tense.

_____

_____

_____

_____

4. <u>Release:</u> Create your own personal Visual Release Imagery and Release Statement to be used every time you go through this process. It is important that both the visual imagery and the release statement are the same every time you use them. First visualize your release image. Then write your Release statement down below.

e.g. I am visualizing my sadness and anger being packed up in a hot air balloon and floating away, or I am visualizing my anger being burned in a beautiful outdoor campfire. Release Statement: *I am free of this sadness. I no longer need this feeling. I let it go with love.*

Image:

Statement:

PERSONAL EMPOWERMENT PROGRAM – WEEK 5:

REFRAMING THOUGHTS

The principles of cognitive therapy are simple. *We are constantly thinking. Our thoughts create our emotions. Often, our thoughts are simply not true. And even if they are true, we can find a way to reframe them into a better feeling thought.*

For each major thought we have, use this simple exercise to reframe our thoughts. Make sure you have completed the Processing Feelings worksheet first, however, as it is imperative that we feel our feelings before we can release them.

1. **List the primary thought that seems to be causing emotional pain.**

    e.g. I am fat and unlovable.

    _____

    _____

    _____

2. Ask yourself the simple question: Is this thought true? (even if you answer yes, proceed to the next questions.)

e.g. Well ok, not totally true because I'm not like really fat and some people do love me like my parents and my friends. So no, I guess that thought isn't true.

_____

_____

_____

3. Ask yourself: How would I feel without this thought?

e.g. I would feel much better about myself if I really believed it. I wouldn't be so down all the time and I wouldn't be thinking about food and exercise all the time.

_____

_____

_____

4. Reframe the thought.

   e.g. I am healthy and people do love me.

   _____

   _____

   _____

5. Repeat the reframed thought internally as an affirmation until the negative sentiment behind the thought is lifted.

PERSONAL EMPOWERMENT PROGRAM – WEEK 6:

FIND YOUR HIGHER POWER

The good news is that nobody knows for sure what, who or how a Higher Power/God may operate in this world. Therefore, you can simply design your own higher power that works for you and has your best interest at heart. This exercise asks you to create a personal ad for your own personal Higher Power. Just like a match.com ad for a romantic partner or a wanted ad in the classified section of your paper, outline the qualities you want in your Higher Power.

e.g. Must be all forgiving, loving, kind and compassionate. Will listen to everything that is on my mind and provide loving and supportive answers. Does not punish or seek to make me feel guilty. Loves everyone and everything. Understands when I make mistakes and loves me anyways. Is beautiful and a spark of my Higher Power is in everyone and in everything. Is most easy to access in quiet and in nature, but is really everywhere all the time. Loves me unconditionally.

My Want Ad for my Higher Power

_____

_____

_____

_____

_____

_____

_____

_____

_____

_____

_____

_____

_____

_____

_____

_____

_____

_____

_____

_____

Now just simply choose to believe that the very Higher Power you asked for has responded and works in your life just as you requested.

PERSONAL EMPOWERMENT PROGRAM – WEEK 7:

DISTINGUISHING BETWEEN HAPPINESS AND JOY

What we call happiness is often the result of attaining external things that bring us contentment, i.e. a massage, a tall drink after work, a dinner at a nice restaurant, praise from our boss, a monetary raise, a new car etc. There is nothing inherently wrong with this external means of happiness, but often the happiness they bring is fleeting and not permanent.

Joy is a result of aligning your actions with your values. Joy results from doing things that make you feel good about who you are and what you bring to the world, i.e. volunteering at the homeless shelter, finishing my college degree, taking care of my adopted shelter dog, running a marathon This exercise is designed to help you distinguish the things in your life that bring you happiness and bring you joy. The long-term goal is to continue to add to the Joy list to experience more long-term lasting fulfillment.

10 things that bring me happiness:

1.

2.

3.

4.

5.

6.

7.

8.

9.

10.

10 things that bring me JOY:

1.

2.

3.

4.

5.

6.

7.

8.

9.

10.

PERSONAL EMPOWERMENT PROGRAM – WEEK 8

DEATHBED EXERCISE

Take a moment to still your mind through deep breathing and quiet. Imagine you are peacefully aware that you have only weeks or months to live. Your life has been incredibly rich, full, meaningful, and you are left feeling as if you have zero regrets for the life you have lived. You are at complete peace because you absolutely know that you lived the life you were meant to live. Now take a moment to write down your reflections on the particular areas of your life.

Accomplishments/Bucket List: List the things that you presently hope to accomplish, places to visit, etc. before you reach that peaceful place at the end of your life.

1.

2.

3.

4.

5.

6.

7.

8.

9.

10.

11.

12.

13.

14.

15.

16.

17.

18.

19.

20.

You may need to add many more to this list. Or your list may be shorter as you have already accomplished most of what you desire.

Relationships healed: Think of any unhealthy present relationships in your life and identify how you would hope to think about these relationships on your deathbed. If there are actions you need to take to rectify the situation, list below. Or if there is simply healing that needs to happen in your heart, identify that as well.

Who:
What:

Who:
What:

Who:
What:

Who:
What:

Eulogy

Write your own eulogy. Outline what to you would make you feel as if you lived a life of meaning and purpose.

Life 101 Personal Notes and Reflections

Life 101 Personal Notes and Reflections

Life 101 Personal Notes and Reflections

Life 101 Personal Notes and Reflections

ABOUT THE AUTHOR

Ashley Anne Connolly is a licensed psychotherapist living in Aspen, Colorado with her husband and two young boys. She earned her undergraduate degree from Northwestern University and her Master's degree in Counseling Psychology from Loyola University Chicago. She is the author of *"The Course They Never Offered in College: Reflections on A Course in Miracles for Young Adults"*, *"Dear Sweet Baby James: Spiritual Musings From a Mother to Her Newborn Son"*, and many feature articles in *Enlightened Women Magazine*. Ashley is a competitive runner, a skier, a spiritual seeker, and an ardent believer that emotional wellness is the cornerstone to a good life.

ACKNOWLEDGEMENTS

- ❖ To Mike, James and Win for giving me my beautiful life.
- ❖ To Mom for always showering me with unconditional love.
- ❖ To Dad for teaching me to have fun and to "Go For It."
- ❖ To Gary for being a constant steady and steadfast support.
- ❖ To B for being an amazing mentor in every aspect of my life.
- ❖ To my friends traveling on the spiritual journey with me.
- ❖ To my Higher Power for Everything.
- ❖ To the many inspiring authors, teachers, institutions, psychological and spiritual traditions that have influenced my life in deep and profound ways:
  - ○ A Course in Miracles, Science of Mind, Paramahansa Yogananda & the Self-Realization Fellowship, Mile-Hi Church, The Aspen Chapel, Hay House, Bill

W. & Dr. Bob, Wayne Dyer, Cheryl Richardson, Tama Kieves, Louise Hay, Marianne Williamson, Glennon Doyle Melton, Brene Brown, Shefali Tsabary, Oprah Winfrey, Martin Seligman and Positive Psychology, Harmony House, Northwestern University, Loyola University Chicago and the Institute of Transpersonal Psychology.

With Love and tremendous Gratitude,

xoxox

Ashley

Ashley

Made in the USA
San Bernardino, CA
29 November 2016